Secret
Destinations

Secret
Destinations
Charles Causley

PAPERMAC

First published 1984 by Macmillan London Limited

First published in paperback 1986 by
PAPERMAC
a division of Macmillan Publishers Limited
4 Little Essex Street London WC2R 3LF
and Basingstoke

Associated companies in Auckland, Delhi, Dublin, Gaborone,
Hamburg, Harare, Hong Kong, Johannesburg, Kuala Lumpur, Lagos,
Manzini, Melbourne, Mexico City, Nairobi, New York, Singapore
and Tokyo

British Library Cataloguing in Publication Data

Causley, Charles
  Secret destinations.
  I. Title
  823'.912   PR6005.A837

ISBN 0-333-42507-3

Printed in Hong Kong

To
Michael Hanke

Note

A number of these poems were written
while I was writer-in-residence at the
University of Western Australia, at the
Footscray Institute of Technology,
Victoria, and with the Music Theatre
Studio Ensemble at the Banff Centre,
Banff, Alberta. To all these institutions,
and to the Literature Board of Australia,
I should like to express my thanks for
their encouragement and support.

C.C.

Launceston
Cornwall
February 1984

Contents

'All journeys have secret destinations of which the traveller is unaware.'

Martin Buber

Sorel Point

The rocks, of child's red plasticine,
Blister the sea's strong glass. A pair
Of gulls switchback on curving air.
Thin water yeasts the faultless sand.
Dressed for the day and Sunday-clean
The quarry's hurt, salt-washed and dried,
Spills its neat gut down the cliff-side.
In whitest white and blackest black
The shore-light turns its iron back
On the small sureness where we stand.

Hand on the rail, I lean down to
The almost out-of-earshot bay;
The taut horizon's silver-grey
Disseverance of blue and blue.
I turn to you, but you are gone
Up the hung path of whitened stone
To where your wife and children wait.
Now dispossessed of the great sea
A stranded tide snakes under me.
Translate, I hear you say. Translate.

Seven Houses

To David English

This is the house where I was born:
Sepulchre-white, the unsleeping stream
Washing the wall by my child bed.
I shall outlive you all, it said.

This is the house where I was born:
Its eastward pane a rose of light,
A water cross upon my brow
Pointing a path to day from night.

This is the house where I was born:
A spoil of children; and where grew
A bough of words; and printed birds
Awoke, and shook their wings, and flew.

This is the house where I was born:
A dripping mill; a bed of grain;
A voice that said, 'Now you shall know
The gate of blood through which you came.'

This is the house where I was born:
A sea that writhed beneath the floor
And stood upright upon the sands
And beat the door with deep, green hands.

This is the house where I was born:
The silky waters of the bay
A shroud for ships' bones, and a long
Brown garden, dry with insect song.

This is the house where I was born:
Where in the white drifts of the moon
First words, like snowflakes, touched the page
And stayed, unfaded, with the noon.

'Which is the house where I was born?'
I asked the true and turning stream.
That house, the water said, *is known
Only when life is told and done*:

*A roof upraised; a stair half-grown,
Willed to the starving rain and sun;
A scuttled wall; a founding-stone;
A house that never was begun.*

Grandmother

Rises before the first bird. Slugs about
In gig-sized slippers. Soothes the anxious whine
Of the washing-machine with small bequests
Collected from our room. Whacks up the blind.
Restores a lost blanket. Firmly ignores,
With total grace, your nakedness. And mine.

At seven the kitchen's a lit quarter-deck.
She guillotines salami with a hand
Veined like Silesia. Deals black, damp bread,
Ingots of butter, cheese, eggs grenade-strong.
Thinks, loudly, in ground German. Sends a long
And morning glance across anonymous crops
To where the *autobahn*, fluent with cars,
Spools north to Frankfurt, and unpromised land.

The clock, carted from Prague, hazards an hour.
A neighbour's child appears, failed priest at eight
In shirt and table-runner; ruptures mass
From *Hänsel und Gretel*. Does his holy best
To trip her. Filches sugar, sausage. Spoils
Her apron-strings. She lets it all go by
With the same shrug she gave when the burst car
Refused to let us vamp it into life,
And her to church. Perhaps it was the same
In Hitler's thirties: the Sudeten farm
Left in a moment, and her history
Carried in paper bags beneath each arm.

Her face is like a man's: a Roman beak
Caesar might quail at; and the squat, square frame
An icon of compassion. As she turns
Towards the leaning light, behind her eye
Burn embers of Europe's foul allegory.
Her body bears its harsh stigmata, dug
With easy instruments of blood and bone.
And still, I'm certain, she could up and stick
A yelling pig, a priest, a partisan
With equal mercy. Or a lack of it.
She's wise as standing-stones. Her gift of years
Almost persuades belief in God, the Devil;
Their parallel unease. Both heaven and hell
Entirely unprepared for her arrival.

Richard Bartlett

Reading the ninety-year-old paper singed
By time, I meet my shadowed grandfather,
Richard Bartlett, stone-cutter, quarryman;
The Bible Christian local preacher, Sunday
School teacher and teetotaller. *Highly*
Respected, leading and intelligent
Member of the sect. He will be greatly missed.
Leaves wife and family of seven children,
The youngest being three months old.

Nine on a July morning: Richard Bartlett
About to split a stone, trying to find
A place to insert the wedge. The overhang
Shrugs off a quiet sting of slate. It nags
Three inches through the skull. Richard Bartlett
Never spoke after he was struck. Instead
Of words the blood and brains kept coming.
They lugged him in a cart to the Dispensary.
Never a chance of life, the doctors said.
He lived until twelve noon. His mate, Melhuish,
Searched for, but never found, the killing stone.
The fees of the jury were given to the widow.

The funeral was a thunder of hymns and prayers.
Two ministers, church-yard a checkerboard
Pieced with huge black: the family nudged nearer
The pit where the Workhouse was, and a leper's life
On the Parish. And in my grandmother
Was lit a sober dip of fear, unresting
Till her death in the year of the Revolution:
Her children safely fled like beads of mercury
Over the scattered map. I close the paper,
Its print of mild milk-chocolate. Bend to the poem,
Trying to find a place to insert the wedge.

Dora

My last aunt, Dora Jane, her eye shrill blue,
The volted glance, the flesh scrubbed apple-clean,
Bullets for fingers, hair cut like a man,
Feet in a prophet's sandals, took the view
That work was worship; kept a kitchen share
In this her book of very common prayer.

She never called me Charles. Instead, the name
My father went by: Charlie. Who brought home
The war stowed in his body's luggage; died
In nineteen twenty-four. The strong wound bled
Unspoken in her heart, no signal tear
Disburdened on a waywardness of air.

One tale she prised from childhood. Prised again.
A brother and two sisters. How they ran
To the high field, through the tall harvest sea,
The stolen matches for a summer game.
As it was born, each pretty painted flame
Matching the sun's fire. And how suddenly

The youngest was a torch, and falling, falling,
Swathes of her long hair, and her burned voice calling.
Indifferent, the sun moved down the day:
The boy, my father, beating hand to bone
On the hard flame that struck a breath away
And turned a body and blood to a black stone.

Caught in her trap of years, Dora still told
Her tale, unvarying as granite. Held
Life at arm's length. And there were lovers, though
The clear blue gaze killed questioning. Revered
The tarot pack, fortunes in tea-cups. Feared
Nothing when it was time for her to go;

Half-smiled at me as sentimentalist.
The biscuit-tin clock thumping by her bed
Placed so that she could see the day drawl by.
Our only death, said Dora, is our first.
And she turned from me. But her winter eye
Spoke every word that I had left unread.

Uncle Stan

Here's Uncle Stan, his hair a comber, slick
In his Sundays, buttoning a laugh;
Gazing, sweet-chestnut eyed, out of a thick
Ship's biscuit of a studio photograph.
He's Uncle Stan, the darling of our clan,
Throttled by celluloid: the slow-worm thin
Tie, the dandy's rose, Kirk Douglas chin
Hatched on the card in various shades of tan.

He died when I was in my pram; became
The hero of my child's mythology.
Youngest of seven, gave six of us his name
If not his looks, and gradually he
Was Ulysses, Jack Marvel, Amyas Leigh.
Before the Kaiser's war, crossed the grave sea
And to my mother wrote home forest tales
In Church School script of bears and waterfalls.

I heard, a hundred times, of how and when
The blacksmith came and nipped off every curl
('So that he don't look too much like a girl')
And how Stan tried to stick them on again.
As quavering children, how they dragged to feed
The thudding pig; balanced on the sty-beams,
Hurled bucket, peelings on its pitching head –
Fled, twice a day, from its enormous screams.

I watched the tears jerk on my mother's cheek
For his birth day; and gently she would speak
Of how time never told the way to quell
The brisk pain of their whistle-stop farewell:
A London train paused in the winter-bleak
Of Teignmouth. To his older friend said, 'Take
Good care of him.' Sensed, from a hedging eye,
All that was said when neither made reply.

I look at the last photograph. He stands
In wrinkled khaki, firm as Hercules,
Pillars of legs apart, and in his hands
A cane; defying the cold lens to ease
Forward an inch. Here's Uncle Stan, still game,
As Private, 1st Canadians, trimmed for war.
Died at Prince Rupert, B.C. And whose name
Lives on, in confident brass, for evermore.

That's all I know of Uncle Stan. Those who
Could tell the rest are flakes of ash, lie deep
As Cornish tin, or flatfish. 'Sweet as dew,'
They said. Yet – what else made them keep
His memory fresh as a young tree? Perhaps
The lure of eyes, quick with large love, is clue
To what I'll never know, and the bruised maps
Of other hearts will never lead me to.
He might have been a farmer; swallowed mud
At Vimy, Cambrai; smiling, have rehearsed
To us the silent history of his blood:
But a Canadian winter got him first.

The Boot Man

'Thin as sliced bacon,' she would say, fingering
The soles. 'They're for the Boot Man.' And I'd go
Up Crab Lane, the slight wafer of words she doled
Me out with worrying my tongue. *Please, soled
And heeled by Saturday.*

                    She didn't know
That given speech, to me, refused to come.
I couldn't read aloud in class; sat dumb
In front of howling print; could never bring
On my bitched breath the words I should have said,
Though they were pummelling inside my head.

Somehow the Boot Man stanched my speeches more
Than all the rest. He'd watch me as I tried
To retch up words: his eyes a wash-tub blue,
Stork-head held sideways; braces threaded through
Loops in his long-johns. Once again my dead
Father stood there: army boots bright as glass,
Offering me a hand as colourless
As phosgene.

               And they told me time would cure
The irresolute tongue. But never said that I
Would meet again upon the faithless, sly
And every-morning page, the Boot Man's eye.

1940

June 13th, nine forty-five, the train
Seething. Tin adverts warming in the sun:
Monkey Brand Soap, Zebo, Sanatogen,
An empty chocolate-machine, its tongue
Stuck out. Beside the signal-box a blend
Of serious flowers. Torn posters: a North Coast
Too-sweet with light, 22-carat sand,
Edged by unhungry seas. In second-best,
Glassed in the space between two lives, we test
The anxious air; file third-class cases on
The rack; observe the engine shake out pure
Blots of black water from its belly. Learn
Our travel-warrants off by heart. Wait for
The land to move; the page of war to turn.

On Launceston Castle

Winded, on this blue stack
Of downward-drifting stone,
The unwashed sky a low-
Slung blanket thick with rain,
I search the cold, unclear
Vernacular of clay,
Water and woods and rock:
The primer of my day.

Westward, a cardiograph
Of granite, Bodmin Moor;
Its sharp, uncertain stream
Knifing the valley floor.
Ring-dove and jackdaw rise
Over the blackboys' bell;
Circle, in jostling air,
The town's stopped carousel.

The quarry's old wound, plugged
With brambles is long-dry.
Dark bands of ivy scale
The torn school; lichens try
The building on for size.
Beyond the weir, a rout
Of barrack-tinted homes
Cancels a meadow out.

Down from the ribbed hill-crest
Combers of grasses ride.
Poppy, valerian
Bleed by the lean lake-side.
Allotments, in a slum
Of weeds and willows, keep
Scrupulous house. I note
A pinch of cows, of sheep.

Vociferous with paint,
A flock of ploughs supplies
Unlocal colour, where
The shut pond slowly dies.
Below the morning's saw-
Edged scope of birches, pines,
The hour is alchemised.
The hurt sun mends. It shines.

This was my summer stage:
Childhood and youth the play,
Its text a fable told
When time was far away.
But once I was too young
And still am too unsure
To cast a meaning from
The town's hard metaphor.

I cannot read between
The lines of leaf and stone,
For these are other eyes
And the swift light has gone.
By my birth-place the stream
Rubs a wet flank, breaks free
From the moored wall; escapes,
Unwavering, to sea.

At the Church of St Anthony, Lisbon

Plump as a Christmas chicken, Fra Antonio
Throbs in the north aisle at a beach of candles;
Clutches, as hand luggage, a conker-coloured
Bible; three little sparking lilies. Handles
His uprising cooler than airline captains: dealing
One foot towards the faithful, a long gaze
Past the chipped saints and the once-painted ceiling
Up to the time-burnt dome, flayed pink and blue,
The burst glass, and the sharp light squinting through.

Tricked by an autumn change of clock, we come
To Mass an hour too soon. A sacristan
On saint-duty points, wordless, to the birth-
Place, marbled wall to wall, and scrubbed
Vanilla-white. It's like a hospital
For sin. Smells wickedly of wax. We scan
Pencilled memorials, prayers, winking stones.
The reliquary's heart of yellow bone
Bays like a brass-section. No sense of loss
That the saint's tongue is in another place.

Blessèd St Anthony, the silver speaker,
Patron of firemen, preacher to Muslims, fishes:
Who asked for, and received, nothing: for whom
The wild ass knelt before the Host as witness
To Christ within the Eucharist: eldest son
Of chaste St Francis, who woke in a vision,
The Child Jesus in his bright arms – the heart
Shies at the thought of your incarnate tongue,
Its taste of iron, of flowers, on my own;
My disbelief, its quiet comfort, gone.

In Padua the day you died, the children
Ran the white streets. Cried, 'Anthony is dead!
Our father Anthony!' And at your sainting
Bells rang, unbidden. On this Lisbon morning,
The Tagus furling into the quick bay,
A donkey, ballasted with guttering, passes.
Neither the time nor place for miracles!
It stops, but not to kneel, before the Host
Of huge stone over me. No magical
Message from Padua; the unpulled bells
Silently lurching high above my head.
St Anthony, our father, is not dead.

Gudow

The road frays to a halt. A dyke
Of little frogs and Indian ink
Right-angles it. A ladder pinked
Half-wasting to a tree swings like
The hanged man. Restless, overhead,
A bird-hide drifts apart. A glass-
Faced cabin points to a distress
Of weeds and wildflowers, thickets mad

With recusant birds. Beyond a snarl
Of wire a parapet bleeds red sand
Where markers prick it. And beyond
Again, a top-shaped tower, a slick
Of nettle and thorn, short bushes thick
With rattled wings, and grasses tall
As children. Through rain-needled air
The guards return our level stare.

Just visible, a small platoon
Of enemy cows moves forwards, back-
Wards through the mist's soft wall. A stick
Bursts underfoot. 'Morgen!' a road-man
Calls to the unseen wire patrol.
Grins, 'Never a reply.' The spring, meanwhile,
Advances, and the death-defy-
Ing cuckoo, heedless, beats the sky.

The Fiddler's Son

When I was a little lad
I lay within the cradle,
But through the living street I strolled
As soon as I was able.

There I met the King's young daughter,
She, too, walked the street.
'Come in, come in, little son of a fiddler.
Play me a tune sweet.'

It lasted scarcely a quarter of an hour.
The King he saw me singing.
'You rogue, you thief, what is that song
That to my child you're bringing?
In France there is a gallows built
Whereon you'll soon be swinging.'

In but the space of three short days
I had to climb the ladder.
'Oh give to me my fiddle to play,
For I'll not play hereafter.'

Then bowed I to, then bowed I fro,
On all the four strings telling.
A fine death lament played I,
And the King's tears were falling.

'My daughter is yours, little fiddler's son,
So to your bride come down.
In Austria is a castle built,
And you shall wear the crown.'

Anonymous
translated from the German

Friedrich

Friedrich, at twenty-two,
Sumptuously bankrupt.
Bought a garage:
Every fuel-tank ailing.

Also a mobilization
Of motor-bikes. Owes
A butcher's ransom
Of Deutschmarks. Has bikes

In the bathroom, kitchen,
Closets, bedroom.
To use the landing lavatory you have
To aim between two Suzukis.

He's a graceful mover; slim as
A fern-tree. Has a dancer's
Small bottom. His wife Peachy's
A sorceress. They don't

Say much when I'm around
But I know they've something
Going between them better than
Collected Poems, a T.S.B. account,

Twelve lines in *Gems*
Of Modern Quotations
And two (not war) medals.
Today, Friedrich

Sat for three hours
Earthed by the ears
To a Sony Sound System.
I couldn't hear

The music, only
Him singing. It was like
A speared hog. *Love,*
Skirled Friedrich, *'s when a cloud*

Fades in the blue
'N there's me, 'n there's you.
'N it's true.
Peachy brings in coke

And Black Forest *gâteau*.
Their mutual gaze
Broaches each other's eye.

Next week he'll be Vasco da Gama.

New Year's Eve, Athens

Outside, Greek snow. I saw you in your room
Face-down, asleep. In black. An unstirred bed.
A figure measuring a marble tomb;
Like our respective loves, already dead.

The Greek Experience was packed and gone:
The sad, stilled caïque in Constitution Square
Rigged with toy lights, aground on paving-stone;
Dancing with cold beside its keel, a pair

Of stranded saints, each one a Nicholas
With boughs of red balloons, where yesterday
Tanks grumbled; resurrecting sentries pass-
Ing in and out of standing coffins grey

As brains or as bad thoughts; the women gift-
Wrapped for Epiphany: furs, patent-leather;
Poseidon's windy shrine in white sea-drift;
Byron's name scraped against the hurling weather;

High, unsweet goat-bells, and the shepherd's clear
Transistor clinking in the grove; the sure,
Strong silences of Delphi that declare
What should be, must be on the listening air.

Suddenly, thunder, and a midnight gun,
Stuttering rockets, shouts and songs. And then
Byzantine bells, jerking in unison,
Urged the year's breath. Whispered, 'Begin again.'

Sleeper in a Valley

Couched in a hollow, where a humming stream
Hooks, absently, sun-fragments, silver-white,
And from the proud hill-top beam falls on beam
Laving the valley in a foam of light,

A soldier sleeps, lips parted, bare his head,
His young neck pillowed where blue cresses drown;
He sprawls under a cloud, his truckle-bed
A spread of grass where the gold sky drips down.

His feet drift among reeds. He sleeps alone,
Smiling the pale smile that sick children wear.
Earth, nurse him fiercely! He is cold as stone,
And stilled his senses to the flowering air.

Hand on his breast, awash in the sun's tide
Calmly he sleeps; two red holes in his side.

translated from the French
of Arthur Rimbaud

Singing Game

The Round House, *c.*1830, is built over a broken
market cross at Newport, Launceston, in Cornwall.

Here we go round the Round House
In the month of one,
Looking to the eastward
For the springing sun.
The sky is made of ashes,
The trees are made of bone,
And all the water in the well
Is stubborn as a stone.

Here we go round the Round House
In the month of two,
Waiting for the weather
To thaw my dancing shoe.
In St Thomas River
Hide the freckled trout,
But for dinner on Friday
I shall pull one out.

Here we go round the Round House
In the month of three,
Listening for the bumble
Of the humble-bee.
The light is growing longer,
The geese begin to lay,
The song-thrush in the church-yard
Charms the cold away.

Here we go round the Round House
In the month of four,
Watching a couple dressed in green
Dancing through the door.
One wears a wreath of myrtle,
Another, buds of thorn:
God grant that all men's children
Be as sweetly born.

Here we go round the Round House
In the month of five,
Waiting for the summer
To tell us we're alive.
All round the country
The warm seas flow,
The devil's on an ice-cap
Melting with the snow.

Here we go round the Round House
In the month of six;
High in the tower
The town clock ticks.
Hear the black quarter-jacks
Beat the noon bell;
They say the day is half away
And the year as well.

Here we go round the Round House
In the month of seven,
The river running thirsty
From Cornwall to Devon.
The sun is on the hedgerow,
The cattle in the stream,
And one will give us strawberries
And one will give us cream.

Here we go round the Round House
In the month of eight,
Hoping that for harvest
We shall never wait.
Slyly the sunshine
Butters up the bread
To bear us through the winter
When the light is dead.

Here we go round the Round House
In the month of nine,
Watching the orchard apple
Turning into wine.
The day after tomorrow
I'll take one from the tree
And pray the worm will do no harm
If it comes close to me.

Here we go round the Round House
In the month of ten,
While the cattle winter
In the farmer's pen.
Thick the leaves are lying
On the coppice floor;
Such a coat against the cold
Never a body wore.

Here we go round the Round House
In the month of eleven,
The sea-birds swiftly flying
To the coast of heaven.
The plough is in the furrow,
The boat is on the strand;
May I be fed on fish and bread
While water lies on land.

Here we go round the Round House
In the month of twelve,
The hedgers break the brier
And the ditchers delve.
As we go round the Round House
May the moon and sun
Guide us to tomorrow
And the month of one:
And life be never done.

Night before a Journey

Books on the printed wall
Withhold their speech;
Pencil and paper and pen
Move out of reach.

The longcase clock in the hall
Winds carefully down.
No matter, says the house-ghost.
He is already gone.

A flower fallen on the shelf,
The stain of moon, of sun,
A wine-glass forgotten –
All await the return.

Nothing in the stopped house
Shall unbalance the air.
There is one, says the house-ghost,
Who is always here,

Patiently watching, waiting,
Moving from room to stilled room,
Light as breath, clear as light.
This, too, is his home.

When shall we meet, the stranger
And I, one with another?
When you leave for the last time,
Says the house-ghost. And together.

Magpie

'Good morning, Mr Magpie. How's your wife
Today?' I say. Spit on the risky air
Three times. The domino-coloured bird skips off
Through lodgepole pines, dry leaves of aspen poplar
Crisping the path.
                              You throw your head back, wear
For a splinter of time my hand in yours, and laugh
Aloud. And suddenly you say, 'You know
Aspen and poplar are the first to grow
After a fire?'
                              The Celt in me, unsafe
Before the magic bird, is hauling up
A rhyme from childhood. *One for sorrow, two*
For mirth. Three for a wedding . . . . 'Magot pies'
Macbeth called them: they point out murderers,
Whose touch makes murdered blood flare out again.

The sun swims down the altered mountain; roughs
A gold line round your head. A wail of box-
Cars threads the valley as I try to scrape
My hand of blood, watching the magpie's track.
He struts in the dust. Bullies a whisky jack.

Flying

Flying over the crumpled hide of Spain,
Seville to Barcelona, the pinned-out skin
Curing in dusty light, I watch a thin
Skein after endless skein of road, mule-track
Thread the wild secrecy of valleys, lap
Impossible hills, and on the sudden plain
Meet other paths; as swiftly part again.

The Moorish castle spoils above the town.
Houses, spilt sugar-lumps, coagulate
Around a church half-eaten by sun. A neat
Gethsemane of olives, grey as slate,
Spreads like a shadow. Stubs of rock stitch lean
Watercourses, sand-beds, in slanting heat.
The land aches with the first green thrust of wheat.

So much to blunt the eye! And still I hear
The squealing bands behind the *pasos*: stare
At porters shouldering wounded Jesus down
Holy Week; the unblemished penitents,
Masked, in fools' caps; the Holy Virgin fenced
By thickets of candle-flame, her shaken crown
A foliage of stars, her wax tears spent.

The ladder-man adjusts the soldier's lance,
Re-lights dead candles, fixes Pilate's cloak.
Crowds flood the Avenida like a dam.
I squat by the cathedral on a rung
Of broken stone. And suddenly the young
Gypsy from the Trianas, peddling coke,
Smiles frankly, makes to pass me by, but first
Runs through me with brilliant, uncasual glance.
Sees me for what I was, for what I am.
Offers a cup. Having observed my thirst.

Bankhead

Under Cascade, its burn of ice,
We saw, as the swift day shut down,
Bitten in sandstone and black shale
The image of the vanished town.
Bankhead! The mine stopped like a tooth;
The unmade engine-house a mix
Of little stones and children's bricks;
Torn rail tracks, giant cacti; paths

From nowhere to nowhere; a scar
Of soil where a church stood, a school.
A burst lamp house. Then becomes now.
No sound but a thin creak of air.
The slow Albertan sky empties
Itself of light, slag-coloured. Trees
Shade into rocks and tipple. A steel
Bin offers its green gape to spill

The careful history of a town
Scraped like a polyp from the skin
Of Canada: of seven seams
Coiled in the land; a winter's tale
Subtle as methane, friable
As the coal, as love; of strikes, bad pay;
The homes at fifty dollars a room
Sold off, like hope, and sledged away.

Miners in tunics, caps, weighed down
With buffalo-horn moustaches gaze
Unsmiling from a photograph:
A vaguely military pose
With safety lamps. Two men stretch out
In foreground dirt like odalisques:
And every face an actor's mask
Hiding incertitudes of heart.

And still the valley dries the print
Of wounds upon its shroud of stone.
Impassive as Stoney or as Cree
The stiff rockface looks sheerly on.
Over the ridge there falls the grey
Cold voice of the coyote. As
I turn to touch your hand, your face,
I know such words as I might say
Must break like glass. And as we go,
Upon the vigilant mountain grow,
Unwatched, the first frail leaves of snow.

Under Mount Rundle

Here comes the little Cornishman, steering
West over the hard swamp and sedge, by winter
Birch and willow. 1841. He wears
Lamb's wool next the skin, a muster of shirts,
Lined trousers, leggings, pilot-coat, moccasins,
A sealskin cap screwed down against the weather.
He is the Reverend Robert Terrill Rundle
Aged 29: 'young, inexperienced,
Of no obvious fitness for his calling.'

His loves are missionising and the mountains.
Born, Mylor, parish of ilex, oak and water.
He flags a mile behind the sled; is disconcerted
At scrawls of blood on the snow from the beaten huskies;
At the delegation of Blackfoot – 'so blackly painted
In history' – that greets him with kisses, prayers: the left
Hand given 'because it is nearest the heart.' The snow
Scores its harsh testament on the plain; goes missing.
He reads. Walks into the broken jaw of the Rockies.

Hussar

Leaving Drumheller, a draft of desert air
Hustling the tumbleweed over the badlands;
Crossing the Red Deer River by the Atlas Mines,
Stone hoodoos stiff as mushroom-hatted janizaries
Slightly askew but braced for arms inspection,
The canyon in three flavours of red, green, gold,
We slithered the dirt road into corn country,
Grain silos in pastel colours, horizon of milk-cartons
Small convoy of houses chancing the plain: R.C. church,
The Christmas lights at the ready in a smoulder
Of afternoon sun, four children thumping a ball,
Two dogs. At the settlement's rim, a sign blaring
Silently. *Hussar. Cultural Centre of Western Canada.*
The sky, the heavy light, pressing the pointed stake
Unremittingly into place; also the one gravestone,
A single tooth in the long yawn of the cemetery.

Untitled

That slender boy of fifteen
in a soft *sfumato* of crayon,
cap dragged down to his eyebrows,
eyes moist and still – his irises dark
and shy; those cheeks dusty as the skin
of apricots; this long-haired Euryalus
perfumed with lemon, needs his Nisus,
but fate has assigned him to a different
day, where, mildly confused, timid and
drowsy, he now poses before Raphael,
to become an ephemeral drawing,
a self-indulgent *ritratto di sé medesimo
quando giovane*, even though the painter
was all of 27 years.

> *translated from the Serbo-Croatian
> of Hamdija Demirović*

Legend

Snow-blind the meadow; chiming ice
Struck at the wasted water's rim.
An infant in a stable lay.
A child watched for a sight of Him.

'I would have brought spring flowers,' she said.
'But where I wandered none did grow.'
Young Gabriel smiled, opened his hand,
And blossoms pierced the sudden snow.

She plucked the gold, the red, the green,
And with a garland entered in.
'What is your name?' Young Gabriel said.
The maid she answered, 'Magdalen.'

Returning South

Five days since I left Cornwall. Sunday bells.
The moor scraped with a February dole
Of sun. Road-signs to Glastonbury, to Wells
Vague with snow-fume. The cold hunch of Brent Knoll
Heavily salted. Fields white as the pole
Through Wiltshire. Then on the windscreen a slow
Small-change of copper-coloured mud. Heathrow.

A Qantas strike. We're ten lost tribes, and tote
Our luggage round the clanging hall as though
Panzer divisions were at the gate.
I dump bags at the check-in. Scratch a note
Already written to no matter who.
Swallow a Scotch. Am launched too late, too soon
At forty-five degrees against the moon.

Bahrain. The sun-god floats above the town.
Eden of poets, pearls! I squinny at
Sumerian verse on plastic tablets. Two
Young sheikhs in lily robes come willowing down
The stairs. Next flight, Damascus. A prayer-mat
Wags from the airport mosque. I wander through,
Touching a silence radical as dew.

At Singapore a steam-iron heat: a scald
Cooling to Melbourne, where we rise, undead,
Above unintimate squares of green and red.
City in hock: near-prisoner of the bald
Shine that's Port Phillip Bay. Unjacketed,
I chuck cash, keys on the still-falling shelf.
Unpack shirts, socks. *Dear Christ, what's this? Myself.*

Beechworth

Stepping out of the sun's clear tide,
Shaking off drops of light, of heat,
The cellar's dark-blue box of air
Envelops me, tempers my cheek:
A drift of air thinned from the Pole,
Although the month is March, and the
Australian autumn newly-born,
Thumped on the bottom, given safe
Conduct to swift, reluctant life.

Behind the grille, a dusty show
Of handcuffs, helmets, an off-white
Anthology of emu bones,
Tin boxes, lamps, a Cobb & Co.
Coach ticket: Melbourne–Bendigo.
The thick bole of an Albion press
Turns, slow as iron, into Zeus
Aiming a finger at the small
Set-piece: a granite prison-cell.

Through a locked door of chicken-wire
A sick bulb challenges the sun
A step away, and corpse-cold air.
And there – My God! But how the heart
Suddenly jars! – a figure lies
In primrose light on an old bed:
A boy, asleep, under a loam-
Grey blanket; the sham, black-haired head
Sharp-angled from the body's frame.

A presage innocent, unspoken,
Of the death-mask, and how the rope
Squirmed tight-shut underneath an ear:
'The bulge shows where the neck was broken';
A rusty bucket, poised between
A chair, a child's white, chipped commode;
A twist of stairs that leads up to
The court-house. A card makes it plain:
'Kelly first gaoled here, aged sixteen'.

Outside, I quietly resume
The sun, among a tarnish of
Rakes, harrows, boilers long unboiled,
Stilled engines – the heart's engine still
Hurrying. Don't want to wake him's my
Excuse, or wake within myself
The necessary response, or hear
The head's dark question, and the sly
Evasions of the heart's reply.

Days drop like leaves; silt the fine shaft
Of years from here to Melbourne Gaol.
I pick a smash of mirror up.
It shows me who I'm not; hides what's
To be, as Ned's epiphany
Burns pure as wax. He rises. Sings.
Stands, noosed and white-capped, on the drop.
Adjusts the rope's scarf. Declares, *Such
Is life*. But knows that it is not.

Pinchgut

Soon after Hiroshima
Three dozen years ago
(As might be three dozen thousand)
Upping and downing past the Heads
Into Sydney Harbour
Eyes on the bridge's grey protractor
Laid against the city and the sky,
I missed a sight of Pinchgut
The broad-arrow island where convicts
Putrefied or, attempting to escape,
Were shark-snapped or strangled
By ropes of water.

This morning, my back to the giant
Hand of oyster-shells
Jammed in a cement beach
(Today, *Madame Butterfly*)
I glimpse the punishing lump
As I take the ferry
To Manly Fun Pier:
Famed for Fun since '31,
Seven miles from Sydney
And a thousand miles from care.

Three trainee-nuns in white and blue
Congeal on a life-raft
Out of the sun's blast
Under a health warning:
Kiss a non-smoker
And enjoy the difference.

I am seeking a sign.
Any kind of sign.
I lurch the deck,
Legs throbbing in concert with the Diesels.
A wartime unease
At skimming over the slum roofs of the sea
Threatens a return.

On the bulkhead a moving hand has written,
Jesus jogs.

The Dancers

To a clearing
in the foyer
at the Gallery
of Art,
and a chatter
of spectators
waiting for the show
to start,
five young men, black,
naked, dotted
white and daddy-long-
legs thin
out of forty
thousand years of
dreamtime came lightfoot-
ing in.
     Ssss! hissed the dancers from Arnhem Land.

And a primal
stillness fell as
when arose the earl-
iest sun,
each dancer an
emblem painted
on rockface, or scored
in stone.
With an unpre-
meditated
seemliness they took
the floor,
staring sightless
as is lightning
through a bronze by Hen-
ry Moore.

Ssss! hissed the dancers from Arnhem Land.

To an insect
buzz of music,
snap of sticks, high nas-
al whine,
touched with brown and
saffron ochre,
and their teeth a yell-
ow shine,
five young men came
barefoot, dancing –
the sun halting in
its climb –
effortlessly,
forwards, backwards
through the littoral
of time.
　　　Ssss! hissed the dancers from Arnhem Land.

Beaded and in
feather bracelets
to the hoarse-voiced didge-
ridoo,
they were emu
and echidna,
swirling snake and kang-
aroo;
razoring this and
that way sharply,
swifter than the bush-
fire flame,
each a demon,
each an angel,
each a god without
a name.

Ssss! hissed the dancers from Arnhem Land.

Suddenly the
dance was ended,
clocks took back the Mel-
bourne day,
and it was as
if the dancers
melted like a mist
away.
In the restaur-
ant I saw them,
serious, and at smil-
ing ease:
five young men in
T-shirts, jeans, with
pavlovas and five
white teas.

   Ssss! hissed the dancers from Arnhem Land.

In a Melbourne Suburb

'The last hot day,' the Italian fruiterer said,
Proving his own bad grapes. Carlton in March.
A Wedgwood sky. Façades of houses whorled,
Fluted like plaster wedding-cakes, and scabbed
Pure black. Bristles of grass. A hand-out, whirled
By traffic says, 'Save Carlton,' but from what
Is not vouchsafed. Cacti, caged and half-caged
On balconies surrender bits of flesh
To sidewalks. Cartons, tickets, coke tins scurf
The road's hard scalp. What passes as a bed
Of white flowers on waste-sprinkled ground takes off,
Lands, and re-forms: squadron of silver gulls.
In autumn gardens khaki campbells pray
From plastic pools for rain. Two Yugoslavs
Sweat out Saturday's footy, as the sound
Of children singing 'Mrs Murphy's Chowder'
Seeps from a junior school. I seat myself
Beneath this vast, anonymous, southern tree.
Think: now's the time to catch a poem; search
For bait; remain relaxed; prepare to cast
A blue line on the afternoon's clear page.

The last hot day. Too soon the swivelling breeze
Assumes another course; from north, from south.
The warm springs of the heart begin to freeze;
The lip and tongue quietly dry with drouth.
High overhead renaissance clouds drift by
In line along an overspread of sky.
I reel the bare catch in. It is the same.
A voice from half a world away. A name.

Greek Orthodox, Melbourne

The church leaks yellow light; a scent
Of drooling wax. A priest hurls in,
Suddenly pitches his black tent,
Scolds God in Greek. The skewer-thin
Acolyte in red trainers tugs
His lace aside, chews gum, prepares
White smoke. Christ from his icon stares
Sightless at ribbons, painted eggs
Smudging in children's hands. Outside,
Circus-high on a rainy tower,
The priest appears bearing the fire,
And Christ is risen. Bells collide
Not quite together. Handshakes, smiles,
Embraces as the last tram fails
To make the depôt, braked by strong
Prayer and thunderflash; a ring
Of dancers. Rockets rip the dark
Sky's cloth. The stems of candles spark
Into gold flowers: each careful flame
Shielded and carried wavering home
For the year's blessing and Christ come.
The church, bricked-out in patterns of
The cross, glows like a lantern. I
Watch the white walls, the rising sky,
How every coloured window prints
Brash histories of death and love.
Nothing is there of certainty.
Ah, how the wicked mosaic glints
In St Nektarios's eye!

Kite, Poisoned by Dingo Bait

Trephina Gorge, Northern Territory

By then the creek had died, and splashed
Sand, fine as pepper, at our feet.
Ghost gums, their leaves nervously green,
Glistened like mercury in the heat.
The gorge opened its wound of rock,
Immaculate in the day's long glare.
Gobbets of stone lay where they fell
In dreamtime through original air.
Liquorice-coloured flies blundered
Expertly, always out of reach.
Wild passion-fruit, half-eaten by
Cockies and ants rubbished the beach.
Spinifex pigeons waddled, swam
From a small shore as bright as bone;
And unsweet in the waterhole:
A cow, its ribs a xylophone.
Wild donkeys, elegantly buffed,
Arrowed a glance and danced away;
Rumped on a naked river gum,
A kite, as motionless as clay.
Plumping its feathers against death
Like northern birds against the frost
It gripped the noon, its eye of stone
Blinded as by a pentecost.

Abandoning the sour pool, we
Slopped through lagoons of desert grit
Back to the truck – ex-Viet Nam,
Still camouflaged – hoping to hit
The beef road to Arltunga. Red
Bulldust made smoke behind us, and
Thinned for a moment, to reveal,
Etched on a plate of scrub and sand,
The cow, heaving comfortably
Into the waterhole. The spry
Donkeys skittering back. The kite
Gleaned from the bough, and shadow-sly
Another in the unversed sky.

Glen Helen

Shaving by torchlight and the webbed window,
Moths butting my lip, my cheek, morning unrisen,
I watch the invisible sky: a graph of dingoes,
Birdsquawk, and donkeys loud as New Year sirens.
The sun inserts a single blade of light
Into the bag of dark; advances low
Over the scrub and sand. Strikes the gorge-side.
It glows in fifty shades of red. The day ignites.

Cardboard cut-outs along the waterhole
Slowly reveal themselves as pelicans.
Divider-stiff, wading birds stab the map
Of corrugated water. The day's finger
Sharpens the skeletons of the ranges: crouched
Frilled lizards, frozen dinosaurs. We pick
Our way among burst cans and cushions,
The carapaces of old cars: pellets
Spat out by delicate monsters. Make a joke
About sand-tires; finding the bitumen.

And underneath our jaunting tongues is this:
How both of us came, hand in cooling hand,
To the stone centre of the wilderness.
Drank from a single cup. Shared fortune; bed.
Pretended not to notice how love bled
Into the eager sand. Lay, heart on heart:
Yet never slept so cold, so far apart.

Alice Springs

A high May sky, pale-blue and faintly brushed
With strokes of cloud. The river-line a gash
Of beer-cans, gums; a froth of broken glass.
A fun-fair grinds the empty afternoon
To months of Sundays, and the fat drunk dances
Silently by the children's carousel.
Anglo-Saxons in shorts and thongs prospect
The flea-market. A black boy (his front-teeth
Removed, therefore initiated) politely
Enquires the time: but time is out of hand,
Lost to bright forces subtler than sand.

Sturt's desert rose: *gossypium sturtii*,
Bakes by the peeling obelisk (part black
Part white), *Lest We Forget*, on Anzac hill.
In the half-fallen sun a doze of camels
Wilting with awful patience. A detritus
Of boomerangs and bells and whips and saddles.
Blow-ups of Afghan drivers, angry-whiskered;
Tribesmen on stilted bones. Landscape: an aching
Pepper of copper-coloured boulders; all
Grown small before the backdrop of the ranges,
The air surly with dust as the light changes.

And in the Pitchi-Ritchi gardens, tablets
To local deities: *Camp Oven Doll,*
Famous for hospitality. Could run up
A Christmas dinner out of mulga bark
And spinifex. Their chariots: *'Pearl of the West',*
Of Western Queensland and the Birdsville track.
Named bullockies who with their teams and wagons
Braved floods and sandstorms and the heat of summer
To keep the town of Stuart (re-named Alice)
With goods from the rail-end at Oodnadatta.

Their names are light; letter by winking letter,
Easing mythologies out of the wild stone,
New dreamtime from a stubbornness of water.

Ross River

Standing at the cabin door,
Morning unlatching the day,
I watch for the timorous
Four-foot lizard's arrival
For a bit of tucker.
The matchbox radio fries up
News from Europe: Death of Tito,
Iranian Embassy Siege Lifted.

Down by the creek, galahs
In primary colours part the simple air
Over the green and yellow Egyptian reeds,
The red wet sand,
Next to a dolour of car bodies,
Gas and beer cans, dead tyres.
Under an awning, Aphrodite,
Beautiful in a washed-out
Khaki shirt and pants
Strips a camp bed, airs the linen,
Is frying bacon: the fat
Explosive as static.

Her young Texan, bush-hatted,
John the Baptist whiskered,
Leads in two camels
He has netted in the Simpson Desert;
Sees the pen in my hand.
'Score, America three,'
He says. 'What's yours,
Poet?'

Echunga

To Jeanne and Brian Matthews

Under a cloister of stringy-barks, rosellas
Dipping in line ahead, an illustration
From a frail map's border, *terra australis*
Incognita, dust jumping where the pick-up
Swats the scraped road, I watch as from an ocean
Of sallow grass the homestead surfaces
Among the masts of eucalypt. Echunga.
A place nearby. Somewhere, buried from sight,
The Murray: 'Come a thousand miles and looks it,'
You say, serving the bread, the white cold wine.

Caught in the early sights of the acacia
I walk the spread. What seems a West Penwith
Light glitters, and the kookaburra seizes
A length of still, blue air; shakes it. Grasshoppers
Flip gracelessly, like brown wood-chips. The sun
Fries down, and skink and stumpytail fluster
From underfoot. Birds on wire twigs abrade
Smooth silences with their complaints. The dam
Opens an oily eye, and at its rim:
Reeds thick enough to hide a Moses in.

A shattered gum lugubriously points
Four ways south, where the sea bites: to a throw
Of homes between us and the pulled-down sky.
Slow rocks turn into drifts of sheep; cattle
Become uneasy stones. Over the hills'
Green barbican, a gulf of carbon where
The bushfire came the day that you expected
The flame to vault the scar; the trees exploding
Ahead of its fast tide. Shadows were blue,
The children told me. Smoke coloured the sun.

And then, you say, just as you all were loading
Paintings, kids' fishing-rods into the car,
Wind and flame suddenly turned, leaving a taste
Of smoke; wry tears wrenched on the cheek.

                                        Today
I see the naked-footed children trawl
The dam for yabbies, and I watch you clinging
Together, minute-long, before I'm driven
Back to the airport. And it is as though
You fear – one, both of you – another kind
Of fire within this Eden, or blood broken
Under the hard sun. The incurious blue, still burning
Over the homestead roof. The sprinkler turning.

Manjimup

We come, the two of us, to Manjimup,
Walking the endless naves of jarrah and redgum,
Shoes smudged with wet loam the colour of blood.
At One Tree Bridge a single kookaburra

Machine-guns the noon light. The cormorant
Casts over the rigid pool its barb of eyes.
Somewhere beyond the rocks and rushes, a bright
Secrecy of maidenhair fern, the stream fidgets

Through sharp stones. We emerge into the kingdom
Of the blue wren, the golden whistler, bees
In a sudden bank of rosemary, curt grasses
Silver-grey, laden with water. The rainbow

Perfect as a child's picture, launches itself
Across a slate sky. 'A nice stand of young karri,'
You say, pointing beyond the jarrah flowing down
The valley towards the hills where the karri begins:

Half-hidden by drifts of blue rain. Ahead,
The blue rain as we move, the two of us, from where
The dryness of jarrah comes to a sudden stop:
You, in another season; I in Manjimup.

Bamboo Dance

They dance, the Filipino boy,
    The Filipino girl, between
The clapping bamboo that would break
    An innocence of blood and bone.

In the hot light, to drum and flute,
    Clear of the bamboo trap they leap.
It is as if they swim in air.
    Music, like water, bears them up.

Barefoot, barelegged, flesh opaline
    As is the secret shell, they move
Their easy bodies to inscribe
    The dusk with characters of love.

And still the bamboo-holders bring
    The poles together like a shot;
Swifter the ever-restless drum,
    The sharp insistence of the flute.

The dance is love, love is the dance
    Though bamboo shocks their dancing day.
Ceases. Smiling, the dancers go,
    Hand locked in gentle hand, their way.

Cottesloe Beach

From India the swimming sea
Touches the shelf of sand,
Gathers a salt, tremendous breath,
Takes a run at the land.
Unceasing on the constant shore
I hear the waters fray,
With rushing speech of stone and shell
Fall back on the bay.

A sky like blacking scrubs the light
Of all but a thin star.
The wind tosses the sheeted sand
Over wire-grass and scar.
I walk the tideline, its rough mark
Of salt and bitter weed.
Shameless, the beach opens its page
For all to read.

At my right hand the sea explodes;
At my left, the tall
Window, bright with ticking flame,
Pictures on the wall.
Someone runs to the mailbox.
A taxi whines by.
Two lovers stand illumined
In its slow eye.

Soon, soon the ocean
Cools the heart's blood to snow;
Blurs with its breath the globe of air
As I turn to go.
Within the sea's dark voice I hear
Another's, long unvisited.
Sleepless, I listen for the light,
The star still glittering in my head.

In the Pinnacles Desert

South of Cervantes, Thirsty Point, wedges
Of capstone galling the track, drumming the gut
Of the four-wheel drive, we cross a sabre-cut
In the scrub. *The Namban River*, I read.
Flows only in winter, ending in a swamp
Near the coast. I raise my eyes. Beyond ridges
Of sand, fine Chinese white, a mess of shell-
Grit, frosted with salt, the sea unrolling
Bolts of long water, and its great bell tolling

Across the Pinnacles, goliath-high,
Facing every which-way. Overhead
A cloud flaps free; spatters pink sand with red.
Here, where the ice-cap melted and returned
Its tithe of water to the sea, the mad
Rocks lean against the wind. They calcify
As ogham stones inscribed by storm and sun;
Bones of the archaeopteryx; the towers
Of mad kings; stairways delicately spun.

Are Easter Island profiles; swollen pin-
Cushions; the improbable arm or hand
Of buried heroes bursting through the sand.
A kangaroo sprints from its scrape of clay.
The emu hunts for seeds. The anchored cray-
Boats swing like metronomes. I see the print
Of the wild-turkey's claw in the dry spine
Of the river-bed first named for Frederick Smith,
Died near this place in 1839

After shipwreck. *Later, re-named Namban.*
The spice-sailors, cruising beyond the reef
Saw a ruined city, and this glittering sheaf
Of stones its monuments. A darkening sun
Slants on the palm, the blackboy tall as a man
Unloosing its gross head of sharpened hair.
Small leaves of rain drift from the sky's tall tree
On the grounded seaman, the failed river named
For Frederick Smith, that will not reach the sea.

At Kennet River

Driving through Separation Creek
I stopped at Kennet River, where
The Tasman in a fury slammed
Breakers house-high upon the sand.

Between the fire-break and the bay
The house took cover from the trees;
The white scent of the eucalypt
Insinuating the salt breeze.

Easter. In the upside-down sky
Fresh wounds of light, and from a far
Ambush of stone a single bird
Scarred with sharp cries the ebony air.

And as I slept and as I woke
A voice within another strove.
'Thus far . . . . thus far . . . .' it seemed to say
In tones discreet and soft as love.

It was the civil-speaking sea
Whispering in its cage of glass,
As night to its new-risen mast
Nailed a rough crucifix of stars.

Early, through Separation Creek,
I went the way that I had come:
The envious flood squirming beside
Me, biding its green tide; its time.

Index of first lines